STOICISM FOR KIDS AND WOMEN

Helping Parents and Kids Thrive while Employing Stoic Philosophies and Tools for Patience, Resilience and Confidence

ANGELINA MARSH

© **Copyright 2021 Angelina Marsh**

All rights reserved. The content contained within this book may not be reproduced, duplicated or transmitted without direct written permission from the author or the publisher.

Under no circumstances will any blame or legal responsibility be held against the publisher, or author, for any damages, reparation, or monetary loss due to the information contained within this book. Either directly or indirectly.

Disclaimer Notice

Please note the information contained within this document is for educational and entertainment purposes only. All effort has been executed to present accurate, up to date, and reliable, complete information. No warranties of any kind are declared or implied. Readers acknowledge that the author is not engaging in the rendering of legal, financial, medical or professional advice.

Please consult a licensed professional before attempting any techniques outlined in this book.

By reading this document, the reader agrees that under no circumstances is the author responsible for any losses, direct or indirect, which are incurred as a result of the use of information contained within this document, including, but not limited to errors, omissions, or inaccuracies.

Table of Contents

Introduction

Stoicism is a school of philosophy that hails from ancient Greece and Rome in the early parts of the 3rd century, BC.

It is a philosophy of life that maximizes positive emotions, reduces negative emotions and helps individuals to hone their virtues of character.

Simply put, Stoicism was designed to help people live their best possible lives.

It's a philosophy of life that maximizes positive emotions, reduces negative emotions and helps individuals to hone their virtues of character.

At any moment, in any situation, and at any stage of life, Stoicism provides a framework for living well. It reminds people of what is truly important, providing practical strategies to get more of what is valuable.

Stoicism was deliberately created to be understandable, actionable and useful. Practicing Stoicism doesn't require learning an entirely new philosophical lexicon or meditating for hours a day. Instead, it offers an immediate, useful and practical way to find tranquility and improve one's strengths of character.

The creation of this guide has these goals in mind.

Stoicism is having a renaissance with entrepreneurs, athletes, and politicians. If you have an interest in learning more about Stoicism, or if you want to explore answers to some of life's most significant questions, please read on!

CHAPTER 1

An introduction to Stoicism

This History of Stoicism

Stoicism is a school of philosophy that hails from ancient Greece and Rome in the early parts of the 3rd century, BC.

It's important to keep in mind how differently people thought then.

People's primary concern was to avoid living an unfortunate life. Therefore, they were more likely to order their thoughts, decisions, and behaviors to promote increased life satisfaction. One of the most important things to keep in mind is individuals didn't automatically assume that they would achieve happiness by attaining money, prestige, and or beautiful things. With great urgency, people wanted to understand how they could have an excellent soul.

Stoicism was one of the famous schools of thought during this period because the Stoics provided compelling answers to anxiety, stress, fear, and troubling questions like "What do I want out of life?" The Stoics offered an operating system that dealt with the trials of the human condition.

Their ultimate answer to all of these issues (essentially) went as follows: I want enduring happiness and tranquility of mind, which come from being a virtuous person.

For instance, a person could hone virtues of character by placing more value on actions over words. In short, positive behavior lead toward a more positive life experience. And, you guessed it-- negative behavior resulted in a more challenging one.

In summation, Stoicism was an ancient school of philosophy that taught a particular way of living. Its principal focus was how to live a virtuous life, to maximize happiness and reduce negative emotions. Its value has been tried and tested over much of human history by renown individuals like George Washington, Thomas

Jefferson, Arianna Huffington, Tom Brady, Tim Ferriss and more.

Its principles may have started long ago, but Stoic strategies are as relevant today as they were in ancient times.

The Stoics

A handful of thinkers helped to form the Stoic philosophy. This section will provide pertinent information about several of the most famous Stoics, as well as what they contributed to the Stoic Philosophy.

Marcus Aurelius

Marcus Aurelius was one of the most influential human beings in human history. He was the head of the Roman Empire for two decades, at a time when it was one of the largest and most influential civilizations the world had ever seen. And despite being an individual of limitless power - who could do whatever he pleased with impunity - emperor Aurelius ardently practiced and lived the Stoic philosophy.

He wrote nightly in his journal about his struggles to live as a restrained, wise and virtuous human being. He wrote them for himself entirely, later his writings were uncovered, collected, and published under the title Meditations. The collection is now recognized as one of the most influential Stoic texts. His writings are a direct look at the thoughts of a practicing Stoic, and he stands as an incredible example of how Stoic strategies can help individuals deal with stressful situations.

Lucius Annaeus Seneca

Lucius Annaeus Seneca was a statesman, a dramatist, and a writer, which gave him real charisma and a way with words. He had a particularly simple, entertaining and memorable way of explaining Stoicism, which has placed his writings among the very best ways for beginners to engage with the philosophy. Also, Seneca's thoughts resonate with modern audiences, due to his unusually practical considerations of topics like friendship, mortality, altruism and the proper use of time.

Zeno of Citium

Stoic philosophy started with Zeno of Citium. Having shipwrecked near Athens, he turned his misfortune into an opportunity by taking advantage of all the philosophical resources available in the city. He sat in on lectures from the other schools of philosophy (e.g., Cynicism, Epicureanism) and eventually started his own. He would teach his theory on the Stoa Poikile (a famously painted porch in Athens), and it is from this Greek word for porch "stōïkos" that the term Stoicism came.

Epictetus

Epictetus, a former slave, improved his station in life to become one of Stoicism's most analytical thinkers. Epictetus' handbook, The Enchiridion, is an especially practical look at how to implement the Stoic philosophy in one's life. He had a particular talent for explaining how Stoic strategies improve one's quality of life and made a compelling case for why one might want to make Stoicism their primary operating system. Many of his teachings have become recognizable, without being known as his.

For instance, one of his principles is at the basis of the: serenity prayer: *"God grant me serenity to accept the things I cannot change, Courage to change the things I can, And wisdom to know the difference."*

Principles of Stoic Philosophy

The Stoic philosophy changed over time, shifting focus from logic and physics - to more psychological concerns like tranquility and well-being. Also, the Stoics could never convene to affirm all of their tenants precisely, but there are certain principles at the core of the Stoic operating system. Here are some of the most important beliefs and strategies that the Stoics recommend to live a better life.

Importantly, these are not just interesting ideas to think about and then forget, they are meant to be practiced every day of one's life.

"Waste no more time arguing what a good man should be. Be One."

– Marcus Aurelius

As the philosophy developed, the Stoics came to have very little patience for purely theoretical contemplation. They focused less on pondering for the sake of it and more on real-world pragmatism.

In the real world, you need to arrive at an answer and take action. A true Stoic is not an "armchair philosopher," but someone who gets out and lives by their theory.

Also in this quote, one can immediately see the Stoic concern for a righteous life. Stoics think that a good life is one of moral action. If you want to live well, you have got to be a morally just person.

"The chief task in life is simply this: to identify and separate matters so that I can say clearly to myself which are externals not under my control, and which have to do with the choices I actually control. Where then do I look for good and evil? Not to uncontrollable externals, but within myself to the choices that are my own..."

– Epictetus

Stoics acknowledge that people don't have control over all, or even much, of what happens in life. And they emphasize that worrying about things outside of their control is unproductive, or even irrational to a person who wants to attain tranquility.

The Stoics would have us remind ourselves daily - to actively differentiate between what is and is not under control - to not waste energy over uncontrollable adverse events.

Where many people worry endlessly about things out of their control, the Stoics think their energy is better spent thinking of creative solutions to problems, rather than the issues themselves.

"No person has the power to have everything they want, but it is in their power not to want what they don't have, and to cheerfully put to good use what they do have."

– Seneca

Living as a Stoic does not mean you must live without material goods. In fact, the Stoics think that material goods are just - to the extent that they serve your happiness and ability to live virtuously.

However, Stoics are hyper-aware of the power of consumerism over their tranquility and decision-making. Many individuals spend a significant portion of their days upset about not having a more beautiful car or a bigger home, even though they have excellent health and more possessions than most.

Seneca was known to practice days of poverty, where he would fast and wear unfashionable clothing, to remind himself that people do not require luxuries to live a good life. All in all, individuals have enough to get by and be happy, yet they are upset about their lives because they maintain an insatiable desire for more.

Stoics consciously try not to suffer over what they lack. Instead, they guide their awareness towards gratitude for what they have.

"I judge you unfortunate because you have never lived through misfortune. You have passed through life without an

opponent—no one can ever know what you are capable of, not even you."

– Seneca

The Stoics take a very different view of misfortune than most people. They expect mishaps and use them as opportunities to hone their virtues. That is not to say that they are glad when troubles beset them, but they try not to lament them needlessly, and they actively seek benefit wherever possible.

Imagine breaking a leg and needing to sit in bed for four months while it heals. A Stoic would attempt to guide their thoughts away from useless "woe is me" rumination and focus instead on how they might do something productive while bedridden (e.g., write their first book). They would try to reframe the event as a way to cultivate their patience and become more creative.

Where there is an adverse event, Stoics try not to let it ruin their tranquility, and instead, they try to derive character-building benefits wherever possible.

"External things are not the problem. It's your assessment of them. Which you can erase right now."

– Marcus Aurelius

The Stoic way of life has made its way into modern Psychology. Cognitive Behavioral Therapy, or CBT, is based on the idea that how we think (cognition), how we feel (emotion) and how we act (behavior) all interact together. Specifically, our thoughts determine our feelings and our behavior. So, Stoicism is an ancient thought that has been proven by modern psychological science!

In many ways, one's thoughts determine their experience of reality. For two people who undergo the same hardship, their differing assessment of that same misfortune can result in entirely different emotions and behaviors. Where one may feel utter despair at the loss of a job, another may feel liberated and hopeful about the opportunity.

Monitoring one's inner critic towards greater optimism can be a boon to psychological well-being. Remember, it is not the event itself that makes one upset, but one's thoughts about it.

"Let us prepare our minds as if we'd come to the very end of life. Let us postpone nothing. Let us balance life's books each day. ... The one who puts the finishing touches on their life each day is never short of time."

- Seneca

"Keep death and exile before your eyes each day, along with everything that seems terrible— by doing so, you'll never have a base thought nor will you have excessive desire."

- Epictetus

 "Memento Mori" has been an important concept in many philosophies, from the Stoics to the Existentialists. It means "remember that you will die." While this may seem morbid, Stoics like Epictetus & Seneca believed that contemplating one's mortality can lead to more gratitude and virtuous action.

Instead of always wanting more, this exercise reminds the Stoic to appreciate what they have, while they have it. Or in other words, Stoic philosophy can help you appreciate good like health and well-being while they have them.

When one remembers that their lives are not infinite, it tends to clarify what is really important. This idea is often summed up as advice given in the form of "You could get hit but a bus tomorrow." Again it seems morbid, but the point is to get out and live today. Don't stress so much about the little things, and ensure that you carpe that diem, as you won't always have another chance.

"The good or ill of a man lies within his own will."

- Epictetus

It ought to be said at least once more - that virtue is the primary concern of the practicing Stoic. More important than wealth or even health, excellence of character is the highest good.

A Stoic thinks that as long as they think and behave virtuously (things which are always under their control), that they need not concern themselves with the impact of external events that lay outside of their control.

Whether or not people are rude or one experiences an unending streak of bad luck is irrelevant, as long as the Stoic responds in virtuous ways - he/she can rest easy in knowing that they're living a good life.

Ways People Practice Stoicism Today

Tim Ferris on practicing famine

"Practicing poverty or practicing rehearsing your worst case scenario in real life, not just journaling, not just in your head, I find very, very important.

For instance, I will regularly, three continuous days per month minimum, practice fasting. I will do that from early Thursday dinner to an early Sunday dinner to simply expose myself to the rather, often unfamiliar, sensation of real hunger.

The more you schedule and practice discomfort deliberately, the less unplanned discomfort will throw off your life and control your life."

-Tim Ferris

Ryan Holiday on the Premeditation of Evils

"Practice premeditatio malorum (a premeditation of evils). Everyone talks about positive visualization.

The stoics practice negative visualization. Think about what could go wrong, accept that it is a possibility, prepare for it, proceed anyway. Don't be caught by surprise by misfortune, be ready for it."

- Ryan Holiday

CHAPTER 2

Stoic Ethics

The tremendous influence Stoicism has exerted on ethical thought from early Christianity through Immanuel Kant and into the twentieth century is rarely understood and even more rarely appreciated. Throughout history, Stoic ethical doctrines have both provoked harsh criticisms and inspired enthusiastic defenders.

The Stoics defined the goal in life as living in agreement with nature. Humans, unlike all other animals, are constituted by nature to develop reason as adults, which transforms their understanding of themselves and their own true good.

18

The Stoics held that virtue is the only real good and so is both necessary and, contrary to Aristotle, sufficient for happiness; it in no way depends on luck. The virtuous life is free of all passions, which are intrinsically disturbing and harmful to the soul, but includes appropriate emotive responses conditioned by rational understanding and the fulfillment of all one's personal, social, professional, and civic responsibilities.

The Stoics believed that the person who has achieved perfect consistency in the operation of his rational faculties, the "wise man," is extremely rare, yet serves as a prescriptive ideal for all.

The Stoics believed that progress toward this noble goal is both possible and vitally urgent.

Definition of the End

Stoicism is known as a eudaimonistic theory, which means that the culmination of human endeavor or 'end' (telos) is eudaimonia, meaning very roughly "happiness" or "flourishing."

The Stoics defined this end as "living in agreement with nature." "Nature" is a complex and multivalent concept for the Stoics, and so their definition of the goal or final end of human striving is very rich.

The first sense of the definition is living in accordance with nature as a whole, i.e. the entire cosmos. Cosmic nature (the universe), the Stoics firmly believed, is a rationally organized and well-ordered system, and indeed coextensive with the will of Zeus, the impersonal god.

Consequently, all events that occur within the universe fit within a coherent, well-structured scheme that is providential. Since there is no room for chance within this rationally ordered system, the Stoics' metaphysical determinism further dictated that this cosmic Nature is identical to fate.

Thus at this level, "living in agreement with nature" means conforming one's will with the sequence of events that are fated to occur in the rationally constituted universe, as providentially willed by Zeus.

Each type of thing within the universe has its own specific constitution and character. This second sense of 'nature' is what we use when we say it is the nature of fire to move upward. The manner in which living things come to be, change, and perish distinguishes them from the manner in which non-living things come to be, change, and cease to be.

Thus the nature of plants is quite distinct from the nature of rocks and sand. To "live in agreement with nature" in this second sense would thus include, for example, metabolic functions: taking in nutrition, growth, reproduction, and expelling waste.

A plant that is successful at performing these functions is a healthy, flourishing specimen.

In addition to basic metabolism, animals have the capacities of sense-perception, desire, and locomotion.

Moreover, animals have an innate impulse to care for their offspring. Thus living in agreement with a creature's animality involves more complex behaviors than those of a plant living in agreement with its nature. For an animal parent to neglect its own offspring would therefore be for it to behave contrary to its nature. The Stoics believed that compared to other animals, human beings are neither the strongest, nor the fastest, nor the best swimmers, nor able to fly.

Instead, the distinct and uniquely human capacity is reason. Thus for human beings, "living in agreement with nature" means living in agreement with our special, innate endowment—the ability to reason.

Theory of Appropriation

The Stoics developed a sophisticated psychological theory to explain how the advent of reason fundamentally transforms the world view of human beings as they mature. This is the theory of 'appropriation,' or oikeiôsis, a technical term which scholars have also translated variously as "orientation," "familiarization," "affinity," or "affiliation."

The word means the recognition of something as one's own, as belonging to oneself. The opposite of oikeiôsis is allotriôsis, which neatly translates as "alienation."

According to the Stoic theory of appropriation, there are two different developmental stages. In the first stage, the innate, initial impulse of a living organism, plant, or animal is self-love and not pleasure, as the rival Epicureans contend.

The organism is aware of its own constitution, though for plants this awareness is more primitive than it is for animals. This awareness involves the immediate recognition of its own body as "belonging to" itself.

The creature is thus directed toward maintaining its constitution in its proper, i.e. its natural, condition. As a consequence, the organism is impelled to preserve itself by pursuing things that promote its own well-being and by avoiding things harmful to it. Pleasure is only a by-product of success in this activity.

In the case of a human infant, for example, appropriation explains why the baby seeks his mother's milk. But as the child matures, his constitution evolves. The child continues to love himself, but as he matures into adolescence his capacity for reason emerges and what he recognizes as his constitution, or self, is crucially transformed. Where he previously identified his constitution as his body, he begins to identify his constitution instead with his mental faculty (reason) in a certain relation to his body.

In short, the self that he now loves is his rationality. Our human reason gives us an affinity with the cosmic reason, Nature, that guides the universe. The fully matured adult thus comes to identify his real self, his true good, with his completely developed, perfected rational soul. This best possible state of the rational soul is exactly what virtue is.

Whereas the first stage of the theory of appropriation gives an account of our relationship toward ourselves, the second stage explains our social relationship toward others. The Stoics observed that a parent is naturally impelled to love her own children and have concern for their welfare. Parental love is motivated by the child's intimate affinity and likeness to her. But since we possess reason in common with all (or nearly all) human beings, we identify ourselves not only with our own immediate family, but with all members of the human race—they are all fellow members of our broader rational community.

In this way the Stoics meant social appropriation to constitute an explanation of the natural genesis of altruism.

Good, Evil, and Indifferents

The Stoics defined the good as "what is complete according to nature for a rational being qua rational being" (Cicero Fin. III.33). As explained above, the perfected nature of a rational being is precisely the perfection of reason, and the perfection of reason is virtue.

The Stoics maintained, quite controversially among ancient ethical thought, that the only thing that always contributes to happiness, as its necessary and sufficient condition, is virtue. Conversely, the only thing that necessitates misery and is "bad" or "evil" is the corruption of reason, namely vice. All other things were judged neither good nor evil, but instead fell into the class of "indifferents." They were called "indifferents" because the Stoics held that these things in themselves neither contribute to nor detract from a happy life.

Indifferents neither benefit nor harm since they can be used well and badly.

However, within the class of indifferents the Stoics distinguished the "preferred" from the "dispreferred."

(A third subclass contains the 'absolute' indifferents, e.g. whether the number of hairs on one's head is odd or even, whether to bend or extend one's finger.)

Preferred indifferents are "according to nature." Dispreferred indifferents are "contrary to nature." This is because possession or use of the preferred indifferents usually promotes the natural condition of a person, and so selecting them is usually commended by reason. The preferred indifferents include life, health, pleasure, beauty, strength, wealth, good reputation, and noble birth.

The dispreferred indifferents include death, disease, pain, ugliness, weakness, poverty, low repute, and ignoble birth. While it is usually appropriate to avoid the dispreferred indifferents, in unusual circumstances it may be virtuous to select them rather than avoid them. The virtue or vice of the agent is thus determined not by the possession of an indifferent, but rather by how it is used or selected. It is the virtuous use of indifferents that makes a life happy, the vicious use that makes it unhappy.

The Stoics elaborated a detailed taxonomy of virtue, dividing virtue into four main types:

- wisdom
- justice
- courage
- moderation

Wisdom is subdivided into good sense, good calculation, quick-wittedness, discretion, and resourcefulness. Justice is subdivided into piety, honesty, equity, and fair dealing.

Courage is subdivided into endurance, confidence, high-mindedness, cheerfulness, and industriousness.

Moderation is subdivided into good discipline, seemliness, modesty, and self-control. Similarly, the Stoics divide vice into foolishness, injustice, cowardice, intemperance, and the rest.

The Stoics further maintained that the virtues are inter-entailing and constitute a unity: to have one is to have them all. They held that the same virtuous mind is wise, just, courageous, and moderate. Thus, the virtuous person is disposed in a certain way with respect to each of the individual virtues. To support their doctrine of the unity of virtue, the Stoics offered an analogy: just as someone is both a poet and an orator and a general but is still one individual, so too the virtues are unified but apply to different spheres of action.

Appropriate Acts and Perfect Acts

Once a human being has developed reason, his function is to perform "appropriate acts" or "proper functions."

The Stoics defined an appropriate act as "that which reason persuades one to do" or "that which when done admits of reasonable justification." Maintaining one's health is given as an example. Since health is neither good nor bad in itself, but rather is capable of being used well or badly, opting to maintain one's health by, say, walking, must harmonize with all other actions the agent performs.

Similarly, sacrificing one's property is an example of an act that is only appropriate under certain circumstances. The performance of appropriate acts is only a necessary and not a sufficient condition of virtuous action. This is because the agent must have the correct understanding of the actions he performs. Specifically, his selections and rejections must form a continuous series of actions that is consistent with all of the virtues simultaneously. Each and every deed represents the totality and harmony of his moral integrity. The vast majority of people are non-virtuous because though they may follow reason correctly in honoring their parents, for example, they fail to conform to 'the laws of life as a whole' by acting appropriately with respect to all of the other virtues.

The scale of actions from vicious to virtuous can be laid out as follows:

1. Actions done "against the appropriate act," which include neglecting one's parents, not treating friends kindly, not behaving patriotically, and squandering one's wealth in the wrong circumstances;

2. Intermediate appropriate actions in which the agent's disposition is not suitably consistent, and so would not count as virtuous, although the action itself approximates proper conduct. Examples include honoring one's parents, siblings, and country, socializing with friends, and sacrificing one's wealth in the right circumstances;

3. "Perfect acts" performed in the right way by the agent with an absolutely rational, consistent, and formally perfect disposition. This perfect disposition is virtue.

Passions

As we have seen, only virtue is good and choiceworthy, and only its opposite, vice, is bad and to be avoided according to Stoic ethics. The vast majority of people fail to understand this. Ordinary people habitually and wrongly judge various objects and events to be good and bad that are in fact indifferent.

The disposition to make a judgment disobedient to reason is the psychic disturbance the Stoics called passion (pathos).

Since passion is an impulse (a movement of the soul) which is excessive and contrary to reason, it is irrational and contrary to nature.

The four general types of passion are:

- distress
- fear
- appetite
- pleasure

Distress and pleasure pertain to present objects, fear and appetite to future objects. The following table illustrates their relations.

Table of Four Passions (pathê)

	Present Object	Future Object
Irrationally judged to be good	Pleasure	Appetite
Irrationally judged to be bad	Distress	Fear

Distress is an irrational contraction of the soul variously described as malice, envy, jealousy, pity, grief, worry, sorrow, annoyance, vexation, or anguish.

Fear, an irrational shrinking of the soul, is expectation of something bad; hesitation, agony, shock, shame, panic, superstition, dread, and terror are classified under it.

Appetite is an irrational stretching or swelling of the soul reaching for an expected good; it is also called want, yearning, hatred, quarrelsomeness, anger, wrath, intense sexual craving, or spiritedness.

Pleasure is an irrational elation over what seems to be worth choosing; it includes rejoicing at another's misfortunes, enchantment, self-gratification, and rapture.

The soul of the virtuous person, in contrast, is possessed of three good states or affective responses (eupatheiai). The three 'good states' of the soul are

- joy (chara)
- caution (eulabeia)
- wish (boulêsis)

Joy, the opposite of pleasure, is a reasonable elation; enjoyment, good spirits, and tranquility are classed under it.

Caution, the opposite of fear, is a reasonable avoidance. Respect and sanctity are subtypes of caution.

Wish, the opposite of appetite, is a reasonable striving also described as good will, kindliness, acceptance, or contentment. There is no "good feeling" counterpart to the passion of distress.

Table of Three Good States

	Present Object	Future Object
Rationally judged to be good	Joy	Wish
Rationally judged to be bad	—	Caution

For example, the virtuous person experiences joy in the company of a friend, but recognizes that the presence of the friend is not itself a real good as virtue is, but only preferred. That is to say the company of the friend is to be sought so long as doing so in no way involves any vicious acts like a dereliction of his responsibilities to others. The friend's absence does not hurt the soul of the virtuous person, only vice does.

The vicious person's soul, in contrast, is gripped by the passion of pleasure in the presence of, say, riches. When the wealth is lost, this irrational judgment will be replaced by the corresponding irrational judgment that poverty is really bad, thus making the vicious person miserable.

Consequently, the virtuous person wishes to see his friend only if in the course of events it is good to happen. His wish is thus made with reservation (hupexhairesis): "I wish to see my friend if it is fated, if Zeus wills it." If the event does not occur, then the virtuous person is not thwarted, and as a result he is not disappointed or unhappy. His wish is rational and in agreement with nature, both in the sense of being obedient to reason (which is distinctive of our human constitution) and in the sense of harmonizing with the series of events in the world.

The virtuous person is not passionless in the sense of being unfeeling like a statue. Rather, he mindfully distinguishes what makes a difference to his happiness—virtue and vice—from what does not. This firm and consistent understanding keeps the ups and downs of his life from spinning into the psychic disturbances or "pathologies" the Stoics understood passions to be.

Moral Progress

The early Stoics were fond of uncompromising dichotomies—all who are not wise are fools, all who are not free are slaves, all who are not virtuous are vicious, etc.

The later Stoics distinguished within the class of fools between those making progress and those who are not. Although the wise man or sage was said to be rarer than the phoenix, it is useful to see the concept of the wise man functioning as a prescriptive ideal at which all can aim. This ideal is thus not an impossibly high target, its pursuit sheer futility. Rather, all who are not wise have the rational resources to persevere in their journey toward this ideal.

Stoic teachers could employ this exalted image as a pedagogical device to exhort their students to exert constant effort to improve themselves and not lapse into complacency. The Stoics were convinced that as one approached this goal, one came closer to real and certain happiness.

CHAPTER 3

A Stoic Approach to Parenting

Launching a stoic blog to share ideas on parenting from a Stoic point of view. Today, years later, we need parenting help and support now more than ever as we live through months and months of pandemic lockdowns. Being a mom or dad during the pandemic has become an enormous challenge, beyond what we've ever experienced before in our lifetimes.

Consider these facts:

- We're all doing more childcare at home, whether it's for younger kids or teens.
- Around 40 percent of childcare providers have shut down, and children are at home with their parents.
- Many schools are teaching virtually, and kids need help throughout the day.

- Children can't participate in activities such as sports, extracurriculars, or aftercare programs.
- Some parents are working remotely and trying to keep an eye on kids at the same time.
- Other parents have to cut back on work, take a leave, or even quit.
- Other parents have lost jobs that they didn't want to lose, and they are worried about supporting their families.

So, kids need a huge amount of attention and support right now, and so do their parents.

On top of our current crisis, there's another reason why being a mom or dad has gotten harder: The rise of "intensive parenting." Today, the pressures to help our children succeed are strong.

Studies show that American parents are spending more and more time and resources on extra classes, activities, sports, tutoring, test prep, and more for their kids. This is especially true in middle- and upper-income households.

From my experience with two children in the public schools in a culturally and economically diverse city in California, I see parents of all backgrounds striving to help their kids do well in school and in their future careers. As our kids get older, we all know that colleges have only so many slots and so many scholarships, and that our children are competing with others in our state, our country, and across the world.

So, in the service of "what's best for our children," parents today are tempted to go to outrageous lengths to shape every single aspect of the future for their kids.

As a mom, I, too, have felt the desire to pave the way for my kids to succeed (never using illegal means, thankfully!). But I have realized that this is an impossible—and really a misguided—task. And it is not healthy for me, or my children. Instead, I turn to my life philosophy to guide my parenting: **Stoicism.**

Stoic parenting philosophy focuses on becoming more rational and mindful, and less anxious and controlling as parents, and giving our children more autonomy, especially as they get older.

Above all, we need to always bear in mind two things: what we truly want for our children at a basic level, and the fact that we have the power to not give our assent to impressions or mistaken beliefs based on social pressures. As a mother, what I want most for my children is to help them develop these key things:

- Their character—using the Stoic virtues of practice wisdom, justice, courage, and self-control as guideposts
- Their ability to choose well and make sound judgments after questioning their knee-jerk reactions (questioning their impressions, in Stoic terms)
- Their internal motivation to grow, learn, and thrive—and to act in the world creating positive change as citizens, individuals, and family members

I've explored this in my own life and I've been sharing it. Now, I'd like to expand on a framework for how Stoicism can help us as parents get to a point where we can help our children develop their character in this way and act as a good role model for our kids.

It starts with working on ourselves, especially in relationship to the world of other parents, kids, and society in general. (Note: When I use the words "we," "us," and "our" here, I am thinking of all parents and those in parenting roles.)

First, with Stoic life philosophy, we see that other peoples' opinions just aren't that important.

What's important is living by our ideals and striving for the virtues, finding that moral core. And as long as we are working to develop our faculty of choice, our moral sense, and aiming towards the virtues in our decisions, then we are good, and we are good role models for our kids.

Do we really care what other families post on social media about their vacations, birthdays, fancy material goods, achievements? Should that influence how we spend our time and energy?

Second, as parents, must realize that many, many things are outside our control.

Stoicism's core teaching about "the dichotomy of control" tells us to stop trying to exert control over things that are outside our power. There's so many of these things as a mom or dad.

Here are some of the elements of our children and their lives that we can't control:

- A child's individual personality, abilities, health, and interests
- How a child gets along with other kids, and the friends she or he makes
- The competitive nature of other people/environments
- Deep-rooted structural issues: Inequities in incomes, schools, and opportunities that are difficult to surmount (we may be able to influence this, but can't necessarily change it)

When we think about how we deal with some of the things outside our control, the first line of defense could be to start saying no to the thoughts that pop up about comparison of our kids and our situation with other people's.

Third, as Stoics, we can use our spark of reason to figure out what is in fact reasonable to do as parents to support our kids.

It's always within our power to say no to more activities as a mom or dad, things that just create busyness in our lives. I like to think about what Marcus Aurelius wrote:

"... most of what we say and do is not essential. If you can eliminate it, you'll have more time, and more tranquility. Ask yourself at every moment, 'Is this necessary?'"

—Marcus Aurelius, Meditations, 4.24

For me as a parent, things like bake sales fall into this category. I can say no to those, and make a small donation instead. Or organizing very elaborate parties. Or attending all my daughters' sports practices. I'd like to add: Not doing these things does not make me a terrible mother, just one who is less stressed about being perfect in every way and saying yes to every ask.

I suggest trying to identify the kinds of supportive activities you actually enjoy doing as a parent, and the things that bring you closer to your kids and show them your values. And maybe even are fun.

For example, my husband had the chance to DJ at my daughter's school walkathon fundraiser. He connected with the cause and the kids—who still talk about it. And I serve as a Girl Scout Leader, with over 5 years of volunteering, because I find it provides real character building for my kids—and me—through social service and outdoor challenges.

And I'm always available for are homework help or discussions about friends or debates about ideas or family exercise outings.

Saying no to time-sucking things—for instance things we might be tempted to do just to look good on social media—is strongly supported by Stoicism. As Seneca wrote:

Nothing is ours, except time. We were entrusted by nature with the ownership of this single thing, so fleeting and slippery that anyone who will, can oust us from possession.

Fourth, accepting that our children are not under our direct control is critical.

In a way, it's similar to a teacher and her students. Even Socrates, revered by the Stoics, reported that he had students whose behavior was awful. Well, he said, I don't control their minds. All I can do is provide a role model, and the rest is in fate's hands. As parents we have more influence than a single teacher, but we nevertheless need to accept that there are limits. We still feel a very real sense of duty and responsibility about our children, but we can't expect to mold them into exact replicas of ourselves, let alone better versions of what we hoped to become.

So, to sum up, Stoic philosophy enables me to cope with the pressures parents face today in healthier ways, and I think all parents could benefit from a dose of Stoic philosophy. And I also hope it's helped set my kids on a path of well-reasoned choices that will serve them long into the future.

I've learned a few key things about kids that have helped in this journey, too, that I'd like to share.

As I mentioned earlier, it is important to think about how we can help kids develop their own character with Stoic ideals. First, I'll share some general thoughts, and then I'll talk about a few practical suggestions.

Today, many parents express love through consumerism or entertainment for their children. But the ancient Stoics were a lot tougher on kids. They believed that character is instilled through things like exercise, sports, and hard work. In other words, they thought that we develop virtue through work. So even today, in a Stoic-inspired life, it's more valuable what we give children to do, rather what material things we give to them. And it's also what we show them that we care about, through our own actions, and what we teach them about as role models.

We should give children things to do that require effort on their part, and that are challenging. This could be physical challenges. When our kids express interest in doing something brave, we encourage them to try it.

And on family outings, we try to do something outside of our comfort zone. It might be challenging physically, like hiking through a river or up a mountainside. Or challenging intellectually: museums and historical sites expose children to art, science, and history.

Even if kids aren't enthusiastic at first, they usually learn something. Kids can also work on challenges in our communities and our world by volunteering. Mine have done service projects on pedestrian safety, mental health, feeding families of hospitalized, and helping the homeless.

Things are different today. In a pandemic lockdown with virtual-only school, there are tons of new challenges that are tough for parents and kids, and overall, it's not very positive. The isolation of staying home, rather than attending school or preschool; the need for constant supervision for younger ones; the boredom of staring at school classes on a screen; lack of time with friends and in social settings; temptations of entertainment and video games... and for some, dealing with sickness or financial problems at home.

But while it is very hard for us as parents to watch our kids confront difficult things—and we are dealing with many added burdens ourselves—there might be something of a silver lining.

Maybe it will help our children build character. Because it turns out that recent studies have shown that facing challenges and even feeling uncomfortable can actually be a good thing for kids. In fact, through new psychology research, we are discovering that keeping our kids perfectly protected from any adversity or challenge is actually harmful to them and, long term, it can create anxiety or depression.

The authors of an Atlantic article about this research wrote: *"despite more than a decade's evidence that helicopter parenting is counterproductive... kids today are perhaps more overprotected, more leery of adulthood, more in need of therapy."*

Today, my parenting philosophy is focused largely on autonomy. On raising independent adults.

This approach was intuitive to me, and confirmed once I started practicing Stoicism: The strongest predictor for motivation in kids and teens is a sense of control over their own choices.

A great book on this topic is The Self-Driven Child, by William Stixrud and Ned Johnson. The authors convincingly make the case that today's parents often deprive children of meaningful control over their own lives, putting them at higher risk of anxiety and depression. And they add that parents' own anxiety can harm their children's well-being. They talk about how moms and dads can have a "non-anxious presence" for their kids, and stop micromanaging everything from their homework to their friendships.

As I discussed earlier, I think Stoic life philosophy can inspire us to be less anxious and more present for our kids in the moments when it counts. This is about focusing our attention on what matters, a personal connection to our children, and support for their moral or character development. And that kind of mindfulness and attention are right in the Stoic wheelhouse.

My kids call me or my husband out when we are distracted while we talk (for instance, looking at our phones). I give them credit. Having a family times of day, at dinner, or a family downtime, like a regular game night, helps us be present at specific times.

One other big picture idea about our kids: Let's think about our children's agency.

I've heard it said that Stoicism is a way of maximizing agency. Remember that kids aren't the puppets of their parents, who need to orchestrate their every move. They are people. When they are old enough, they need to learn to make choices and commitments. They have to figure out what motivates them and how to spend their time. This is not easy, but it is worth the effort to try.

We can be good role models in this sense, showing the kids of decisions we make and how we choose to live our lives. And we need to devote time to actually explaining to our children how we arrive at these decisions. It comes down to this: When our children choose, and we are not forcing kids to do things, not saying "do this because I said so," we are giving our daughters and sons a chance to become full people and make commitments of their choosing. And that is a worthy goal indeed.

So, this leads to an important question for Stoic parents:

How should we present Stoic ideas to children?

With children who are very young, their own immediate needs and wants are paramount.

They are driven by hunger, fatigue, play, competition with other kids. They haven't learned to use their reason, or to fully understand cause/effect.

They don't acknowledge others' needs or wishes – they are just too young. But studies in neuroscience show kids aged 7 to 9 are laying the structure for reasoning in their brains, and that they grow these areas a lot at around ages 12 to 13.

I think ages 9 or 10, or possibly as early as 8 or 9, could be a good time to introduce some Stoic philosophical ideas more formally, a few high-level ideas about the dichotomy of control, the three disciplines, the virtues, and questioning or impressions.

But I think we could begin sharing the Stoic approach bit by bit with toddlers. Even at a very young age, we can already talk to our kids about

- the things that are inside and outside of our control;
- about the consequences of our choices;
- explain how to question our impressions—that is, our knee-jerk reactions to things.

I like to say, "Stop, drop, and question your impressions" (even though it's more of a joke in my house, it gets kids' attention!).

For example: One of my children always had trouble leaving playdates when she was a toddler, around age 3. She would get very upset about leaving a friend's house when playtime was over, and she'd refuse to do it. So I started to explain the situation to her, to try to help her understand others' perspectives as well as the consequences of her actions. The host family has their own schedule, I'd say, and that's not in our control. They have to start cooking dinner now. Your response to them is in your control. You can change how you behave.

Remember, you probably won't get invited over here again if you don't leave when you are asked to go. And what if it were our house? And you were hungry? What's in your power to do in this situation?

So you can give your kids a sense for how they could respond, by painting that bigger picture, and using virtues without naming them. I worked on explaining how making a good choice will give them more options in the future.

Another way to help kids gain a Stoic mindset is to give kids simple daily choices, like would you like to eat pears or apples? Peas or sweet potatoes? Just limit it to two or three options at first. Choice is very motivating to children, and we can help them cultivate this faculty.

And for kids' choices, it's good to allow there to be natural consequences so that they can gain some wisdom from it.

For instance, let's say your child refuses to wear a jacket going out when it's 35 degrees outside. If she gets cold often enough, maybe she'll learn to remember her jacket. Or you can spell out the trajectory: "If you don't wear this jacket, you'll be shivering, and you might get sick, and then you'll have to stay in bed all day by yourself instead of doing something more fun this weekend."

I have just one more important point I'd like to make about teaching these principles to children: Stoicism is not about suppressing emotions.

It's about cultivating positive character attributes and virtues, and finding joy, wisdom, and tranquility through making good choices and devoting time to positive things. It's not about pushing down all the things that bother us, deep inside.

With negative emotions, what Stoics call "bad passions," we can use Stoic-inspired CBT-style questioning of misguided beliefs, getting to the root of why we are angry or sad. Then we can try to resolving some of that turmoil by understanding it better, or letting it go. Because it's not the thing that truly matters: it is our moral choices.

Once we realize that others' opinions don't really give us our worth as people, but that our moral core and choices do, we can feel a lot more peaceful. We can try to convey that to our kids too.

Kids who are constantly worried about the judgment of others, in person or online, and be reminded of this principle. People will always be there to be judgmental of us, our parenting, and our kids. To combat the pressure, here is some inspiration from Epictetus:

I laugh at those who think they can damage me. They do not know who I am, they do not know what I think, they cannot even touch the things which are really mine and with which I live.

I'd like to end on a positive note, with the concept of joy. Ancient Stoics were not joyless, and Stoic mindfulness reminds us to live in the present, enjoy spending time with our offspring when they are young or any time, and sampling the "banquet" of life as it comes to us. And that's what this is about: not only the responsibilities that we have towards our kids, but also the joy of having children in our lives.

And when we let go of our controlling or competitive instincts and appreciate our children as human beings capable of developing their own character—as people who will someday become independent adults—we may find that joy comes much more easily.

CHAPTER 4

How To Teach Your Children About Stoicism

The ancients believed that character is fate. That what we are taught when we are young, the lessons we absorb into our DNA, in effect, determines what kind of people we are going to be.

You believe that too. Or you wouldn't be so worried about your kids. The reason you send them to the right schools, why you spend so much time with them, why you analyze and monitor their behavior so closely today is because you know it influences who they will be tomorrow.

It's not a surprise then that one of the most common questions we get is:

How should I teach my child about Stoicism? How can we get our children interested in an ancient school of philosophy? How can we get them to see the value in applying the wisdom of Marcus Aurelius, Seneca, Epictetus, Cleanthes, Chrysippus, and Cato?

How can we develop good character so that all will be well? You've experienced the benefit of this philosophy. You've learned how to reframe obstacles as opportunities. You've learned how to ignore what other people do—their lying, cheating and stealing—and focus only on what you do. You've learned from Marcus how to let go of the dips and valleys of life "with indifference" and accept success "without arrogance." In short, you've learned how to live a good life. And you want to give your children the same experience, only even earlier than you found it.

Thankfully the ancients have some helpful advice for parents. Here are ways to help teach your children about Stoicism:

Start With This Critical Lesson

What use does a five year old have for the concept of philosophy. They don't need to know the name, the dates or even the names of any of the practitioners. Not only are these things confusing, they are inessential.

If I was trying to explain Stoicism to a five year old, I would simply try to convey the most essential piece of wisdom contained inside this robust, complex topic.

I'd tell them: "Look, you don't control what happens to you in life, you only control how you respond."

What do you mean? they'll likely ask.

Here's what we mean: remember when your friend was mean to you last week? That wasn't nice of them, but there also wasn't anything you could do about it. If someone wants to be mean, they're going to be mean. But after they were mean, you had a choice. Remember? You got to decide whether you were going to be mean back, whether you were going to hit them, whether you were going to run to the teacher and tell on them, or whether you were going to just keep playing and forget about it. I know that seems really simple, but it isn't. That situation—when someone does something bad to you and you have to decide how to respond —well, that's life. Adults struggle with it. Even your parents don't always get it right. Even thousands of years ago the Emperor of Rome, a guy named Marcus Aurelius, he struggled with that too.

But the better we can get at it, the happier we'll be and the more fun we'll have and the less sad we'll be. You have that power! You can be as powerful at that king was and as powerful as soldiers and heroes and big strong adults are.

Why? Because you get to choose how you respond to everything. If you can learn that now and embrace it, you'll have the best life ever and no one will ever be able to boss you around. Because you'll be the boss. The boss of your thoughts, feelings and decisions.

Review These Four Virtues

Ok, we've taught them the most fundamental lesson of Stoicism: we have no control over what happens to us—we only control how we respond. This, Epictetus says, is our "most efficacious gift," what distinguishes humans from other animals, the essence of human nature. He calls it the "faculty of choice"—an ability to act rationally, not impulsively, after careful deliberation and assessment.

But how do we know what to choose? How do we evaluate our choices? We shouldn't just choose to do whatever feels natural. Or whatever is easiest. Or whatever everyone else is doing. Thankfully, Stoicism helps us here as well

As Marcus Aurelius wrote:

"Don't be bounced around, but submit every impulse to the claims of justice, and protect your clear conviction in every appearance."

Every day we're tested by impulses of all kinds and faced with these choices. "Think before you act" is a good place to start. But think about what? Marcus would say to start with the four Stoic virtues:

- Moderation
- Wisdom
- Courage
- Justice

These are what Marcus referred to as his "epithets"—the words he lived by, the words that guided every choice he made. "If you maintain your claim to these epithets," Marcus said. *"Without caring if others apply them to you or not—you'll become a new person, living a new life... Set sail, then, with this handful of epithets to guide you."*

As we weigh a choice in response to some event or some opportunity, those are the standards we want to look at.

We want to submit our potential actions to the claims of justice. Is this right? Is this fair? What if everyone else acted as I'm about to act? How would that work out for the world? We want to ask if we're behaving in moderation, if we are being wise, if we are doing the courageous or the cowardly thing.

So teach your kids the four stoic virtues. Return to them frequently. Encourage them to remember the "epithets" they can always fall back on: Moderation, Wisdom, Courage, Justice.

Read Them The Great Books

One of the advantages of the ancient world was that they didn't have so many silly children's books or young adult novels. All they had were what we now call "the classics." So kids weren't just reading silly books about dragons or purple novels about vampires. They were reading and learning from the greatest poets and authors who ever lived—whose books talk about the big issues.

Xenophon, a Greek writer who would go on to be a general and a student of Socrates, recounts a pretty incredible fact about his childhood—incredible for how unremarkable it was for its time. "My father was anxious to see me develop into a good man," he wrote, *"and as a means to this end he compelled me to memorize all of Homer;*

and so even now I can repeat the whole Iliad and the Odyssey by heart."

Can you imagine your kids doing that? The fact that you can't is related to why they can. Your kids will rise to your level of expectations–or at least be improved by trying. Probably not. Do is at least expose them to these classic texts. Don't wait for their school to do it—because they won't (they probably won't even show them the movie either).

In an interview with cognitive-behavioral psychotherapist Donald Robertson about his remarkable book on Marcus Aurelius, How To Think Like a Roman Emperor—in which Robertson artfully weaves in his insight as a working psychotherapist into how the fascinating development of Marcus as a person over the course of his life applies to us today—it was asked that what inspired that unique approach:

"My daughter. I've been telling stories about Greek mythology since she was around three or four years old.

(She's seven now.) The other kids at school talk about their favourite superhero being Batman or Spiderman.

Poppy says her favourite hero is Hercules. Eventually I ran out of stories about mythology and found myself telling her stories about Greek and Roman philosophy...In the ancient world, philosophy was taught through lectures and discussions, and communicated in written lectures, letters, and dialogues like those of Plato and Aristotle.

However, philosophy was also handed down in the form of anecdotes like these, which even a child can learn from. Many of those stories survive today, particularly in a book called The Lives and Opinions of Eminent Philosophers by Diogenes Laertius."

Don't expect kids to find a passion for it on their own, because video games and social media are way easier and more gratifying. You have to teach them. You have to make them excited. Read them stories about the lives of the greats. Read them the great books. The best way to teach your kids about the Stoics is to have them read the actual Stoics!

Learn With Them

Seneca was a father, though we don't know much, if anything, about his son. We know he was a wonderful uncle, and that he struggled valiantly as a tutor to reign in the impulses of Nero. And we know he was a brilliant father to Lucilius, the recipient of Seneca's Letters From a Stoic—which serves as a great example for us parents: You don't have to conduct lectures like Epictetus to be a teacher. Seneca's teaching came in the form of sharing what he was learning.

When you're chauffeuring them around, when you're together around the dinner table, when you're sitting in the waiting room for a doctor's appointment—these are all opportunities to share what you are learning.

I was reading the private journal of the Roman Emperor. You'll never believe what I learned:

- Talk to them about how obstacles can be opportunities
- Talk to them about how we have the power to determine what events mean—that it's not the

events which upset us but our judgments about them).

- Talk to them about the dichotomy of control (as Epictetus said, our first task in life is to determine what is up to us and what isn't)
- Talk to them about the power of memento mori and amor fati.
- Talk to them about the four Stoic virtues
- Talk to them about the fascinating and shockingly modern political dilemmas of Seneca

Seneca wrote in a letter to Lucilius, "I'm talking to you as if I were lying in the same hospital ward." (Which is to say, we're all stuck with the same sickness). Your kids should not think that you're perfect–they should be shown that you're trying to improve yourself just as they are. They should be shown that you guys are actually on the same team. He'd later said, "People learn as they teach."

Scientists, inspired by Seneca's wisdom, have dubbed this The Protégé Effect. Don't lecture them. Learn with them. Read with them. Listen to podcasts and videos with them.

Surround Them With Teachers

It's a scene we all remember from our childhoods. Our parents had a dinner party. Or all the relatives came over for a holiday meal. The kids are put at the "kid table." Or, after everyone had eaten, the kids were sent away. To go downstairs and watch a movie. To put on their pajamas and go to bed. It was "time for the grown ups to talk" and we weren't allowed to be a part of it.

Of course, when we become parents, we instinctively repeat this pattern ourselves. Now that we're the grownups, we're sending our own kids away so we can talk. It makes sense—not everything is appropriate for kids to hear. It feels good to connect with someone our age and at our level sometimes.

But this is a missed opportunity. Benjamin Franklin wrote in his autobiography about his childhood and just how much he benefited from being included in the "grownup" conversation:

"I remember well his being frequently visited by leading people...At his table he liked to have, as often as he could, some sensible friend or neighbor to converse with and always took care to start some ingenious or useful topic for discourse, which might tend to improve the minds of his children. By this means he turned our attention to what was good, just, and prudent in the conduct of life."

Seneca's father selected Attalus the Stoic to tutor his boy. The most powerful lesson that Seneca learned from Attalus was on the desire to improve practically, in the real world. The purpose of studying philosophy, Seneca learned from his beloved instructor, was to "take away with him some one good thing every day: he should return home a sounder man, or on the way to becoming sounder." That's timeless advice that every kid could comprehend and put into practice.

Marcus Aurelius dedicates the entire first chapter of Meditations to his "Debts and Lessons"—seventeen entries reflecting upon what he has learned from various influential individuals in his life. We meet Marcus through his human origins—his parents, his grandparents, his great grandparents, his, his adopted father, and his tutors.

Junius Rusticus, Herodes Atticus, Fronto, Cinna Catulus were all selected by Marcus' adopted father Antoninus Pius to tutor the young boy. In the final entry of that chapter, Marcus thanks "The Gods" for all "the people who brought me up." "I was shown clearly and often," Marcus continues, "what it would be like to live."

And of course there's Cato, who even in his own times, it had become a common expression, "We can't all be Cato's." But where did Cato learn to be Cato? Like Seneca and Marcus Aurlius, his father brought in outside help. A man named Sarpedon, who found the young obedient and diligent, but thought "he was sluggish of comprehension and slow." He was disruptive, not behaviorally. He demanded an explanation for every task and needed to hear a reason for every task that was assigned to Luckily, Sarpedon chose to encourage this commitment to logic rather than beat it out of his young charge. What if Cato didn't have the right teacher?

Let us follow these examples with our own children. Surround them with exceptional influences. If we want to raise grownups, there is no better education than letting them be around grown up conversation. If we want our kids to see the value in philosophy and how it can serve them in their lives, there is no better evidence than the people they look up to displaying that real world application.

Practice What You Preach

Where did Marcus learn to be Marcus? Ernest Renan writes that Marcus was very much a product of his training and his tutors. But more than his teachers and even his own parents, "Marcus had a single master whom he revered above them all, and that was Antoninus."

All his adult life, Marcus strived to be a disciple of his adopted step-father. While he lived, Marcus saw him, Renan said, as "the most beautiful model of a perfect life."

What were the things that Marcus learned from Antoninus? In Marcus's own words in Meditations, he learned the importance of:

- Compassion

- Hard work

- Persistence

- Altruism

- Self-reliance

- Cheerfulness

- Constancy to friends.

The lessons were embodied in Antoninus's actions rather than written on some tablet or scroll. There is no better way to learn than from a role model. There is no better way to judge our progress than in constant company with the person we would most like to be one day.

In his interview with Tim Ferriss, the billionaire Charles Koch explained that the main lesson he learned from his father's very hands-on parenting was that you can't lecture your kids on anything you don't live up to. You can't tell your kids to respect others and then talk rudely to a customer service representative on the phone.

You can't tell them that it's important to find your passion and follow it, and meanwhile work their entire childhood at a job that pays well but makes you miserable. You can't tell them that family is important if your actions don't show it.

It's not that you have to be perfect, but you do have to live up to your own standards—or actively show them what the struggle to get there looks like. Otherwise, you ought to shut your mouth. Because what you're showing your kids is the worst lesson of all: hypocrisy. You're showing them that the principles we claim to hold dear as a society are meaningless, that all you have to do is pay lip service to them, that no one has to actually do anything about them.

Your character forms theirs. You show them who they can be—what they should be. Be who you want them to be. They will follow your lead. Don't lecture your kids. Live the way you want them to live. Live up to your standards, and they'll do the same.

CHAPTER 5

Stoic advice for your children from Epictetus

Let's be honest. As adults and parents, we DO NOT have it all figured out. Just as it has been discussed in the previous chapter. We are not all-knowing, and we certainly aren't perfect. So just because a title of an article makes you think something is advice to your kids, and it is, doesn't mean you can't learn from it as well.

The problem is that many of these life lessons that we as parents learn, are not shared with our kids early enough. Sure, our kids learn more from observations than they do from our words, but it is also effective to share some profound knowledge with them from time to time. When we do, we may actually gain a better understanding of ourselves through the process and create some positive synergy with them.

Epictetus was a stoic philosopher who lived from AD 55 to 135. He believed that philosophy is a way of life. In arguably his most influential work, The Enchiridion, also known as The Handbook, Epictetus taught many lessons about different aspects of life. However, while the knowledge and teachings presented in The Enchiridion were from Epictetus, the writing was actually compiled by his pupil, Arrian. Arrian followed Epictetus around and wrote down many of the words that he spoke. Today, The Enchiridion is held in very high regard by many around that world, and it is still used today to teach and influence many.

The most interesting thing to me about stoicism, and all philosophy, is that the individuals who studied and taught these ideas many years ago were dealing with the same thoughts and issues many of us face today. The times were completely different. Yet through the discovery of America, the growth to 50 states, and the thousands of technological advances, our inner problems as human beings remain constant. The inner struggles that sometimes plague our thinking have never been completely solved.

Thus, the teachings are still relevant today and can be a very useful tool in simplifying our hectic lives.

And yes, our children can learn from Epictetus and other philosopher of the past. Now many of these teachings should be screened by parents before sharing with their kids as they use language and details that were relevant in their time. If taken literally, it is not necessarily the greatest imagery to create in a child's mind. Though the lessons as a whole can be incredibly beneficial, even to kids.

While the life lessons of Epictetus are many, I want to focus on one particular idea that is extremely useful to children in today's world. Here is a quote from The Enchiridion:

Some things are in our control and others not. Things in our control are opinion, pursuit, desire, aversion, and, in a word, whatever are our own actions. Things not in our control are body, property, reputation, command, and, in one word, whatever are not our own actions.

The things in our control are by nature free, unrestrained, unhindered; but those not in our control are weak, slavish, restrained, belonging to others.

-Epictetus, The Enchiridion

Children have a tendency, being raw and innocent human beings, to blame themselves for many of the problems going on in their life. Take, for example, a divorce or custody dispute. A young child stressing through these adult issues invariably blames his or herself for the problems affecting their mom and dad. They often feel like they are the cause of the discord. Another example, on a level of lesser importance, is that children typically blame themselves for the way a coach or teammate treats them on the playing field.

Further, they can feel like a failure if they miss the lay-up or miss the game winning shot.

The problem with this methodology of self-blame and creating worry is that it negatively affects their mindset and their decisions. Also, it is groomed and perfected throughout life. Not only does it cause unneeded stress, but it also forces our children to be predisposed for the future. By the time they get to be adults, they are experts in this field of worrying about things outside of their control. So then, teaching children this lesson from Epictetus is of great importance.

As Epictetus explains, there are things in our control and other things that are not. Simply put, in life there are things that are up to us, and things that are not up to us. Teach your children to only focus on what is up to us, and what they can control. Some things that are up to us include attitude, work ethic, pursuit, desire, perspectives and decisions.

These are really the only things they can control at home, in the classroom, or on the playing field. Things that are not up to us include tragedy, chance, judgments, and reactions of others. The trick is focusing on and perfecting that which we can control, and not being concerned with that which we cannot.

There are many other skills and lessons from Epictetus and other ancient stoic philosophers that we can teach our children. This one in particular could be used as a foundation for the rest of their life. Be concerned about your attitude, not someone's reaction to you. Be cognizant of the worthiness of your decisions, not how someone will think about you. I am not saying they should have a complete disregard for what people think. That is not 100% true. However, they should focus more on having a good attitude and making good decisions based on their own values and learning. In life, if they figure out how to do this as a child, they will be better off than most adults down the road.

CHAPTER 6

How Stoic Parents Raise Boys to Understand

Their Emotions

This is not about maintaining or showcasing masculinity. It's about the emotional wellbeing of our sons.

Gazing into the distance with a cigarette dangling between his lips, the American Stoic is strong, silent, and dying on the inside. He looks like the Marlboro Man. He looks like Alan Ladd in Shane. He doesn't talk much but he gets stuff done. And, after everyone has gone to bed, he sits on the toilet, head in hands, and cries. He does not understand why he is sad. He does not understand why he feels angry and alone. He smokes some more.

The guy who doesn't talk much but gets it done is lionized in America, where men teach their boys to tough it out and pain is just weakness leaving the body. Stoicism, practiced this way, makes a virtue of repression and a mockery of the Roman Empire's non-official, official philosophy.

Which is to say that it's not as strange as it sounds that stoicism is having a minor renaissance. And it's not outlandish as it might seem that there's a three-day camp for Stoics in Hudson Valley, a convention called Stoicon, and multiple websites and Facebook groups devoted to the virtues of "stoic parenting."

Like many American fathers, I've flirted largely unintentionally with teaching my boys about stoicism. Every time my son cries that Ricky tricked him into trading a Pokémon GX for a Raichu or goes full-scale Chernobyl when I ask him to clean up his toys, I am tempted to channel the cut-rate stoicism of my father and say, "How many wah-wahs?" That was the question I used to receive when I was upset. That is how many fathers taught me to hold emotions at a remove or not at all. That is how I wound up spending so much time in therapy learning how to use the tools the real stoics prescribed — the sort of behaviors American adults pay $200-an-hour to learn, but don't teach their kids.

Instead of snapping like my father, Brittany Polat, the mother of three behind the very even-keeled parenting site Apparent Stoic and author of the forthcoming book Tranquility Parenting: Timeless Truths for Becoming a Calm, Happy, and Engaged Parent, recommends that I recall the words of Epictetus. "They have simply gone astray in questions of good and evil," the Phrygian wrote. "Ought we therefore be angry with those people, or should we pity them? But show them their error and you will how quickly they will refrain from their errors."

In other words, says Polat, "No one intentionally makes mistakes. If your son is refusing to clean up his toys, it is because he thinks, mistakenly, it is in his self-interest to do so."

Polat is not asking me to ignore or control my son's feelings, just to understand them in a context and help him achieve that same sort of rational distance from the situation.

Stoics care less about whether you're angry or sad than if you're angry or sad for reasons that make sense.

"That's a very common misconception," says Massimo Pigliucci, a leader in the modern stoic movement and professor of philosophy at City College of New York, "which to be fair has been invited by the Stoics themselves, because of all their talk about controlling negative emotions. But that modifier, "negative," is crucial. The idea has always been to get away from fear, anger, hatred and so on, but also to cultivate joy, love, a sense of justice, and so forth."

The Stoics' poor messaging may be to blame for the modern misinterpretations, but so is time. According to Margaret Graver, a professor of Classics at Dartmouth College and author of Stoicism and Emotion, the issue is in part that philosophy ends up being a bit of a game of telephone if people aren't exposed to original texts.

That's how stoicism became synonymous with emotional suppression despite being a deeply emotional philosophy. "Emotion is a feature of their position," Graver explains. "What is important about human beings isn't that they're emotional, but how well they function as rational creatures, that they are not willing to be deceived."

In other words, Stoics care less about whether you're angry or sad than if you're angry or sad for reasons that make sense.

Graver explains that Marcus Aurelius, Seneca, and Epictetus saw anger as a sign of weakness. "We don't identify what the real threats are because we don't identify our self-interest correctly," she explains, "You get a disjunct between the emotions that are natural and the ones we ordinarily experience."

A philosophy based on rationality clearly has a limit when it comes to dealing with children and the Stoics knew this. Various Stoic texts pinpoint the age of reason at either 7 or 14 years old. But, according to Polat, kids can start to understand the philosophy in practice when they are considerably younger. "I use Stoic principles with my kids all the time, they are six, four, and one," she says. "If my son is crying because he can't find his shoe, I ask him, 'Well, at least a dinosaur didn't eat your mother, right?'" That move, away from the turmoil of the personal and towards broader context, is the Stoic's chief gesture and a profoundly effective way to talk to young boys, who often struggle with self-regulation.

Hierocles, a Stoic philosopher, diagrammed stoic contextualization neatly as concentric circles and called it oikeiôsis. At the center of the circle is the self — or the experience of the self — and at the outer perimeter is the Universe. Stoics and stoic children know that the path towards rationality is the path away from the core experience of emotionality. Thus, the aversion to anger.

If this sounds either radical or antiquated, think again. Oikeiôsis, Pigliucci points out, is the basis of Cognitive Behavioral Therapy, which is a lot more expensive than a copy of Seneca's Letters from a Stoic.

In teaching kids to inspect emotions and then reach for broader context, stoic parents give kids the tools many adults find themselves struggling to develop.

The point isn't to feel along with children, but to understand their feelings and help them cope.

That said, stoicism does run contra to some powerful parenting trends. Mothers and fathers are commonly asked to make sure that kids feel engaged and listened to. Empathy, which Pigliucci refers to as "the e-word," is perceived by many to be a massively important part of parenting. But Pigliucci, who is a father, points out that research doesn't support the idea that empathy is an unqualified good.

"A better approach, which is also the one preferred by the Stoics, is sympathy," he says. "You want to nurture concern for other people, but also keep things in perspective and act reasonably when you are trying to be helpful." He fishes out Seneca to drive home his point: "The first thing which philosophy undertakes to give is fellow-feeling with all men; in other words, sympathy and sociability."

The point isn't to feel along with children, but to understand their feelings and help them cope. Stoics understood this, so much of their work set out various methods and rationales to lessen the intensity of negative emotions and foster the feelings of positive ones. "It is best to think of this as an attempt to shift our emotional spectrum, rather than suppress it," says Pigliucci, "And I think the idea is very much along the lines of the modern psychological concept of raising 'well adjusted' kids." If this sounds great not just for your kids but for you, well, bingo.

"A Stoic attitude helps the parent, not just the child," says Pigliucci, "It is helpful to do daily exercises to control one's anger, to remind ourselves of the big picture, to re-examine our own judgments every night in order to improve them for the next round." In fact, it isn't just helpful but it's necessary too. You can't teach Stoicism by yelling.

Professor Graver provides a great argument for stoic parenting in the form of a personal anecdote. She was shopping up in New Hampshire with her two kids and her daughter was having a meltdown in aisle two. She decided to reason with her. It didn't work immediately, but, eventually, it did work. As Professor Graver checked out, a woman approached her and said, "I really appreciate how patient you are." Professor Graver paused. "Did I have a choice in the matter?" she asked. "How do you manage not to lose your cool?" the woman asked. "Take a realistic and broad view," said Professor Graver before paraphrasing Epictetus, who said, "There are things you can control and things you can't control."

As with all things that parents teach their children, stoicism is best learned by example. If we continue to misapprehend the true lessons of the original Stoics, we'll continue to carve statues of men bluffing their way through their own emotional disconnection. But if we truly understand the words of Epictetus and Seneca and Marcus Aurelius, we can be models. We can teach them, as Marcus Aurelius' father taught him, "manliness without ostentation" or, for that matter, without hang-ups.

CHAPTER 7

4 Things Kids Can Learn From Failure

"Winning isn't everything; it's the only thing."

-Vince Lombardi

I want to make a something perfectly clear at the start. This chapter suggests four lessons that children can learn from failure. However, adults can grab something from it as well. Simply put, anyone who challenges themself in life can learn something from failure, and from this chapter.

Regardless of your outlook on team sports and competition for kids, we should not be teaching our kids that losing can be enjoyable. Can it be beneficial? ABSOLUTELY! But never enjoyable, and a child should not be satisfied with it.

The antidote is Teaching Kids how to deal with Problems.

It's one of the most common questions I hear from parents who are trying to teach their kids Stoic principles: how do I teach my child to deal with frustrations and difficulties? I think this one question goes to the heart of what we do as parents.

Dealing with frustrations and difficulties is a part of every life. It's something our kids must do every day. So, if we can help them develop the skills to successfully face down challenges—and the negative emotions that often accompany challenges—we will be setting them on course for a happier life.

Confronting Challenges

Fortunately, Stoicism is all about confronting challenges. Stoic philosophers provide us with many weapons for dealing with the slings and arrows of outrageous fortune.

For now, I'd like to focus on just one particular psychological weapon that I've found useful for myself and my kids. I call it Apply the Antidote. It's based on the following quote from Epictetus:

"Haven't you been endowed with faculties that enable you to bear whatever may come about? Haven't you been endowed with greatness of soul? And with courage? And with endurance? If only I have greatness of soul, what reason is left for me to be worried about things that may come to pass? What can disconcert or trouble me, or seem in any way distressing?"

In this lecture, a student is complaining about the way his life is going, and Epictetus forcefully sets him straight.

Who are you to find fault with your life? he asks the student. "I can show you that you have resources and equipment that are needed to be noble-minded and courageous, while it is for you to show me what occasion you have for complaint and reproach!"

The message here is clear. Problems are a part of everyone's life. Instead of sitting around whining about it, use the resources and equipment you have to solve the problem. Maybe your nose is running, but you have hands to wipe your nose. Maybe your lamp was stolen, but you can figure out how to get a new one. Maybe you are sick or in pain, but you have the endurance to overcome it.

Let's think about how we can apply the antidote to teach our kids virtue, and then we'll look at how we can use the same advice to become better parents.

Applying the Antidote for Kids

I love this approach to teaching our kids resilience. Instead of just telling them, "Bad stuff happens, get over it," we can emphasize that they have the resources to deal with the problem. When my son falls and scrapes his knee, for example, I can tell him, "I know that hurt, but you are really tough. You can handle it!" I try to identify the particular quality (toughness) that will enable him to overcome that particular problem. His knee might still be hurting, but now he knows that he has what it takes to overcome the pain. He can focus on and be proud of his toughness.

This technique works for most other situations our kids might face. Whenever you are helping them work through a problem, apply the specific antidote that will help them solve that problem. It could be their kindness, intelligence, patience, maturity, or whatever quality you want them to focus on.

When James tries to pick a fight with Clementine, I may tell Clementine, "It's a good thing you are such a big girl. Big girls know not to fight with their little brothers." Or when Freddy takes James' toy: "You are such a kind brother—I'm glad you have such a big heart. You know Freddy is still learning the rules."

Benefits of Applying the Antidote

In case you're wondering if teaching your kids to apply the antidote really helps anything, here are a few of the benefits I've noticed.

- You are explicitly teaching your child the virtues and character traits you value: patience, intelligence, courage, persistence, etc. Be sure you adapt your language to your child's developmental level—use words and concepts she can understand!

- You are helping your child gain confidence that he has actually those desirable virtues. If you consistently remind him that he has the patience to solve the problem, he will start to believe that he has the patience to solve the problem.

- You are preparing your child to work through her emotions on her own. You won't always be standing over your child's shoulder to help out. By talking through this process with her when you are there, you can teach her how to do it for herself when you are not there.

- You are teaching your child to take responsibility for his own emotions. This is one of the most important lessons of Stoic philosophy: we are responsible for our own emotions. Even though we can never solve every problem in the world, we can solve the puzzle of our own emotions. Whether or not the external problem gets "solved," you can still help your child use his own internal resources to overcome anger, frustration, and disappointment.

Applying the Antidote as a Parent

Naturally, as adults we can also apply the antidote to solve our own problems. The best starting point is thinking about the three resources that Epictetus says we possess: greatness of soul, courage, and endurance. I find that whatever problem I am facing, one of those three resources will get me through. When your child is sick, remember that you have the resourcefulness and courage to cope with the situation. When you are sleep deprived and stressed out, you can rely on your endurance to get through it. When your child is testing your patience at the end of a long day, you can rise to the occasion with your greatness of soul. You can always identify some quality that will enable you to bear your burden.

In Marcus Aurelius's Meditations, we see an example of this strategy in action. In Book 9.42, Marcus is working on the difficult problem of unpleasant people. It is impossible that there should be no bad people in the world, he reminds himself. But it is possible for us to deal with them kindly.

To do so, we should reflect on this point: "what virtue has nature granted us to meet the wrong in question? For she has granted us gentleness to use against the unfeeling, and in every other case, another such antidote."

In other words, for every negative action, we can choose an equal and opposite reaction.

We can apply Marcus' antidote anytime we deal with difficult people or situations. Is your toddler having a temper tantrum? Is your teenager slamming the door in your face? Remember the virtues you have to deal with the problem. Does this situation require far-sightedness and understanding from you? Does it require cooperativeness, acceptance, or flexibility? Think about the "equipment" you have to solve the problem. Sometimes you may not be able to solve the external problem in the way you would like to. But you can always solve the internal problem of your own emotions.

When things get tough and you're ready to give up for the day, remember Epictetus' reminder: "You have nobility and greatness of mind to enable you to deal with every circumstance."

CHAPTER 8

Why women should explore Stoicism

Can a woman be a Stoic? "What a ridiculous question," I can imagine debaters on both sides saying. I was reading an old book the other day describing a Stoic woman as a contradiction in terms, like "sweet vinegar." I actually don't think this particular fusty gentleman was being a chauvinist, but rather that he didn't understand Stoicism as well as he thought.

For instance, he interprets Stoicism as being devoid of the elements of compassion and humanity: "It may be well enough to treat things as indifferent, and work them over into such mental combinations as best serve our rational interests. To treat persons in that way, however, to make them mere pawns in the game which reason plays, is heartless, monstrous." I don't understand how anyone can read, for example, Marcus Aurelius for even a minute and not get the sense that the Stoics emphasized caring for other humans.

Not only can a woman be a Stoic, but I would argue that women would particularly benefit from exploring the philosophy. For whatever reasons, men are disproportionately drawn to Stoicism, maybe based on these old, small-s stoic preconceptions described above.

At Stoicon in 2016, the gender balance seemed to be at least 2-to-1 male-to-female. The small-s notion of the emotionless person who forms no attachments conforms better to the over-idealized "strong man" archetype.

Since women are the ones who bear children, and accordingly are associated with the nurturer archetype, the idea of an emotionless woman is distasteful. Luckily, capital-S Stoics can and should have compassion for others.

We all experience emotions; it is part of being human. We all likewise suffer when our emotions take over our rational faculties. By harnessing our emotions into an expression of arete (virtue or excellence), we purify them and put them to good use.

To return to women in particular and what we especially might gain from exploring practical philosophy in general and Stoicism specifically:

Stoicism helps to manage anger

You may have noticed a lot of angry women in the news lately. What are we so angry about all of a sudden?

Nothing . . . we've been angry for a long time. Women are having "a moment," but it's not new.

We are physically weaker–of course there are exceptions, but I'm speaking generally. Men are by and large in charge of things. Oh, and men have the capacity for great violence, often directed at women. Women can be violent too, but I don't think it is too controversial to say that men can do a lot more damage when they become violent. We are currently being governed by a ridiculous man who is taking the saber-rattling to a terrifying new level. So yes, we have a lot to be angry about. Where does it get us? It can be constructive, but it is destructive more often than not. The dichotomy of control–the idea that there are things we can control, and things we can't–can help channel the energy of anger into things we can reasonably influence: our thoughts, our actions, our wishes, our aversions. Actions can certainly include taking to the streets, or leaving an abusive partner, and that would be far more healthy than imploding from anger that is unexpressed.

Lest this revive Nietzsche's criticism of Stoicism as a "slave morality" that merely helps the oppressed come to terms with their shackles, I would emphasize that the dichotomy of control helps us become more proactive in life, not less. By not frittering away our energy on things outside our control, we can focus on actually doing something that is in our purview.

Stoicism helps one feel integrated with the rest of humanity

To say that a woman cannot be a Stoic is to ignore the "circle of Hierocles" which connects everyone to humanity at large via a series of concentric circles, starting small, with the mind, and progressing outward to the immediate family, extended family, local community, and so on until the largest circle encompasses the entire human race. Women, despite all of the changes surrounding gender rights, workplace rights, voting rights, you name it, are still the ones to carry growing humans inside their own bodies. (I have heard of some bizarre exceptions, but let's just say they are statistically insignificant.)

Whether or not you agree that women are hard-wired to nurture the adorable ex-parasites once they emerge, this phenomenon at least insures that women are responsible for nurturing the fetus for ten months, a responsibility that all the pregnant women I have known took rather seriously.

Therefore, many women's alignment with the foundational, small concentric circles of Hierocles is experiential and does not even have to be understood intellectually to be affirmed on a gut level.

As the circles progress outward, however, I suspect many women start to drift from interconnectedness. Many people have commented on the tendency for men to develop many friendships as they go through life–not necessarily deep friendships, but more of a "buddy" relationship. Women tend to make stronger connections with fewer people and do not have as many "buddies."

Moreover, most women would agree that competition among women can be quite fierce. At the same time, relations with men can be fraught. Coupling these two facts means it can feel like a cold world.

Stoicism can help

- eliminate the feeling of competition with other women–after all, we are all behind the eight ball,
- reduce feelings of fear with respect to men.

It is never too late to join the rest of humanity and abandon the state of isolation in which many of us have found ourselves.

Stoicism helps women ignore the "beauty myth"

It has been a while since I read the Naomi Wolf book of the same name, but it had an impact on me. It is common knowledge by now that many women feel societal pressure to be thin and to look perfect. The effort is expensive, time-consuming, and doomed to fail besides, because the concepts of perfect and human are mutually exclusive.

I actually overheard a conversation the other day between two women; one complimented the other for having lost weight, and the other woman said she had the flu and was just now getting her appetite back. The first woman did not say she was sorry her friend had the flu, but instead sounded envious. This is how insane things are. Just think how much more free time AND MONEY women would have if we didn't feel we needed to have perfect hair, abs, butt, skin, and nails, as well as the latest fashions.

Just think how much happier we would be if we would eat a burger when we were hungry, not iceberg lettuce, and had friends who commiserated when we had the flu.

Stoicism is thousands of years old, and immune to fashion trends. It points us in the right direction when societal expectations, our families, our jobs, and our own interests threaten to pull us in many different directions. It is practically free, given the wealth of materials available, and takes very little time to read up on and practice. It gives one a feeling of impermeability in a world that assaults the senses and offends the sensibilities daily.

We can only do so much to change the way things are, but we should take advantage of any tricks to throw off the shackles in our own minds.

CHAPTER 9

Great Insights From Female Stoics

Online (and historically), Stoicism can appear to be a male-bent philosophy. This runs contrary to the fact that one of the founding members of Stoicism, Musonius Rufus, said that to study philosophy is simply for someone to "search out and consider how they may lead good lives." This provoked by the question of whether women too should study philosophy. "Moreover, not men alone, but women too, have a natural inclination toward virtue and the capacity for acquiring it, and it is the nature of women no less than men to be pleased by good and just acts and to reject the opposite of these."

The precedent was set by ancient Stoic women like Porcia Catonis, Annia Cornificia Faustina Minor, and Fannia.

Here are some of their great insights on the role philosophy plays in their search of leading a good life:

***

Renew Yourself Regularly

I have [this quote from Marcus Aurelius] laminated in my wallet, on my desk, and on my nightstand:

"People look for retreats for themselves, in the country, by the coast, or in the hills. There is nowhere that a person can find a more peaceful and trouble-free retreat than in his own mind. So constantly give yourself this retreat, and renew yourself."

It perfectly illustrates the current moment – right now that first retreat he's talking about is mostly digital. That's how we get away from ourselves — by retreating into technology and social media. But the only way to find peace and thrive is to take breaks from the world and make time to regularly renew ourselves by reconnecting with ourselves.

—Arianna Huffington, the founder and CEO of Thrive Global and founder of The Huffington Post.

She has been named to Time magazine's list of the world's 100 Most Influential People and Forbes' Most Powerful

Women list. She is also the author of several bestselling books, including Thrive: The Third Metric to Redefining Success and Creating a Life of Well-Being, Wisdom, and Wonder and The Sleep Revolution: Transforming Your Life, One Night at a Time.

Other People's Opinions

One thing you realize quickly as a female in the music industry is that everyone has a strong opinion about you. It's been my challenge to isolate my view of myself from anything people say about me, the good or the bad.

At the end of the day, none of the criticism or the accolades changes anything real in my life.

To paraphrase Marcus Aurelius, every day we all meet ungrateful, violent, treacherous, envious, uncharitable men. Once you see what sort of person they are, you will realize there is no need to be racked with anxiety that they should hold any particular opinion about you.

I used to love the feeling of proving people wrong, of walking out in front of an audience who expected very little of me and changing their minds.

Now I find myself focused less on proving people wrong, and more on improving myself and my performance.

—Nita Strauss, lead guitarist for Alice Cooper and regularly ranked as one of the best female guitar players in the world.

Managing Feelings

Let us say what we feel and feel what we say; let speech harmonize with life." I find helpful the Stoic notion of indifferent things—all the stuff that doesn't matter or matters a relatively tiny amount, and of thinking through what ideas, including false ideas, my feelings might be based on. It's cognitive therapy but it's also Stoicism.

I also find that reading Seneca can cheer me up, even apart from any ethical or psychological tips I might glean, because his style is so effective; it's absorbing and fun, and it's hard to feel angry or upset when you're busy following a rhetorical avalanche.

A while ago, I re-read Seneca's On Anger during a particularly difficult and enraging time in my personal life, and I did genuinely find it helpful. It's useful to have a reminder of how much being angry can hurt the person who is indulging in the feeling. I try not to be angry, and also not to be passive or ignore what's wrong; it's a tough balance.

I like that Seneca and the other Stoic-influenced writers are so deeply interested in these essential daily questions of how to manage our feelings, and how feelings relate to action.

—Emily Wilson, UPenn Professor and a well-known name in the Stoic community due to her masterful translations of Seneca as well as her biography of the man.

She has most recently made headlines (including The New York Times) with her new, contemporary translation of The Odyssey.

Taming Anger

I'm particularly interested in Stoic accounts of anger. So many of our emotions can be implosive, with most of the real mechanism of them occurring beneath the surface like a serene looking duck whose strange little feet are flapping mercilessly under the water's surface.

Anger is an explosive emotion, meaning that it instantly becomes the problem of everyone else around us. It can also be one of the ugliest and least noble emotions, and is associated with many of the worst errors we make in the course of our lives.

I found Seneca's theory of anger as a misplaced expectation incredibly helpful, and I think of it if I find myself irked by an inability to find my keys, or the less than ideal actions of others. By Seneca's account, anger is not something which happens 'to' us, but an error of basic reasoning. I cannot expect to live in a world where babies don't cry on planes, and I am not entitled to be angry about misplaced keys when I didn't put them back in their usual spot.

Moderating expectation – particularly in relation to things outside of our control, significantly mitigates the impulse to anger, or indeed the experience of the emotion itself.

Emotions — particularly powerful ones — always present themselves within our internal landscape as truthful accounts of that which is external to us.

We think in the moment that we are upset because a colleague said something rude, or that we are angry because someone has treated us unjustly, or whatever.

I'm always struck by Marcus Aurelius' idea that our emotional responses do not exist in any way outside of our internal landscape; they are merely our projection of an external stimulus and the power it holds over us.

The idea that pain, or anger, or any emotion is volitionally manufactured within us, or perhaps volitionally fed by us, is everything that is difficult and wonderful about stoicism.

The responsibility always lies within the individual. This is freeing and irritating all at once.

— Laura Kennedy, freelance writer and journalist based in Dublin, who's earned an enormous following for her thoughtful "Coping" column in The Irish Times, which is based around the everyday usefulness of philosophy

True Happiness

A very common obstacle to true happiness is having a fixed notion of what true happiness is and then aggressively organizing your life to attain this state with all the strategizing, self-management, and personal report cards that go with this happiness-as-target point of view. I don't think happiness can be sought. The seeking, the exertions, the calculating, the trial-and-error, perversely shuts off the happiness spigot.

True happiness, I think, is the meaningfulness that gratuitously happens, shows up, is revealed, or by grace discovered when we fully enter the project of directing our thoughts, words, and deeds toward the good and the worthy. It is in doing this, clumsily, fallibly, and without a compass, but just doing the damn best we can that, in certain moments when are minds and hearts are not defended, we experience love, order, sense, beauty, justice, and all the other ineffable good stuff.

I get out of my head and into my body. I love Stoicism because it values logos, reason, the discerning mind. But I think our minds are often the wisest when we can settle them down to allow new unsought answers in.

I trust the answers that surface during or as a result of my daily yoga practice...I think any daily practice that helps a person withdraw from the noise of everyday life so that wisdom's voice can be heard is valuable.

— Sharon Lebell, philosophical writer and performing musician. Lebell's translation of Epictetus The Art of Living: The Classical Manual on Virtue, Happiness, and Effectiveness—which contains 93 instructions to face each day and the challenges that it presents in a virtuous way— has become one of the bestselling translations of any of the Stoics.

A Global Community

There is a passage of Marcus I often bring to mind. It is fairly graphic and drives home its point vividly:

"If you have ever seen a dismembered hand or food or head cut off, lying somewhere apart from the rest of the trunk, you have an image of what a person makes of himself, so far as in him lies, when he refuses to associate his will with what happens and cuts himself off and does some unneighborly act. You have made yourself an outcast from the unity which is according to nature...you have cut yourself off." (Meditations 8.34, see Stoic Warriors , ch.7.)

The cultivation of empathy is critical, and what Marcus is calling for is a real affective and visceral appreciation that we are citizens of the cosmos or universe.

Respect, for the Stoics, is the cement of the global community. We support and sustain each other...The Stoics were globalists. Their vision of virtue and goodness stopped not individual or small polis, but with the global community."

— Nancy Sherman, Distinguished University Professor and Professor of Philosophy at Georgetown University and an expert on Stoicism in the military, writing the book Stoic Warriors: The Ancient Philosophy Behind the Military Mind.

Overcoming Obstacles

I wish I had stoicism in my life much earlier. It would have gotten me through some pretty tough times. My advice to people experiencing difficulties is, "

Read The Obstacle is the Way by Ryan Holiday"! Seriously! I have recommended your book to many people because of the useful wisdom it offers. Late in the 2015 NFL post-season, I had to work a game in Minnesota in extreme cold — 6-below-zero. I was dreading the game for two weeks.

What was I going to wear? How could I possibly survive the entire game in that temperature? How painful was it going to be? Finally, about five days ahead of the game, I said to myself, "The obstacle is the way. Embrace this challenge. Learn through the preparation. Strengthen my mind through the experience. Collaborate with my on-field team on creative ways to endure. And enjoy the challenge." My anxiety melted away. (See what I did there?? Melted??))

Honestly, the phrase "The obstacle is the way" is one I think about whenever I run into a problem.

— Michele Tafoya, the sideline reporter for NBC Sunday Night Football. The only person to be nominated for the Sports Emmy for Outstanding Sports Personality in all seven years of the award's existence.

She is a powerful advocate for Stoicism and diligent student of the philosophy, as well as a big fan of the Daily Stoic book and regularly shares passages from the book with her followers on Twitter.

Handling Emotions

I think there's a common misconception about Stoicism, that it's about forcing yourself to somehow not feel emotions; that's probably an idea that would appeal more to men than to women (since, from childhood, boys are encouraged to be macho, while girls are encouraged to be in touch with their emotions). But the thing I love about Epictetus is that it's really all about handling emotions.

He's like, "You're definitely going to feel this incredibly powerful thing, but guess what, it's not a law that dictates what you think or how you act—you're perfectly free, and in fact duty-bound, to consult your reason and say, 'OK, feeling, duly noted, but you are just a feeling and not the truth.'" I think that's maybe an especially useful message for women, because of how little girls are educated, or at least how they were when I was little.

I think for a lot of women (as well as men), there's a tendency to think: "Oh my God, I already felt this, so the bad thing already happened." And Epictetus is all about realizing, "Bro, nothing bad has happened yet, everyone has feelings, now just take a moment and evaluate what the truth is.

— Elif Batuman, staff writer for The New Yorker and author of The Idiot, a National finalist for a Pulitzer Prize in fiction.

Agency

"The ultimate test of Stoicism is when you have "hard times." I have had "hard times" and to be honest it isn't as if Stoicism pulled me out of grief or anything like that, but I did not recognize that they were wrong about it either. I was bereft but left with my agency.

What struck me was surprise that more people did not "act out" in grief, with so little left to care about, what would acting terribly matter? It seemed like the Stoic were right that all we really have, since it can be all taken from us in a moment, is our agency and that choice to not lash out when we've been so deeply hurt."

—Jennifer Baker, a professor at the College of Charleston where she teaches courses on ethical and political theory, environmental ethics and philosophy, business ethics, bioethics, and American philosophy.

Her research focuses on virtue ethics, and she looks to ancient ethical theories as positive examples of how ethics ought to be done today. She is also behind the blog "For the Love of Wisdom."

The Power Of Perception

Stoicism entered my life at a very young age without my even knowing what it was. I was a fledging Stoic with a fluffy down of circumstance. I think that we all come into this world natural Stoics, born with no material trappings, just basic needs with patience and acceptance imposed upon us in our moment of birth.

However, focus and will soon kick in! It seems to me that it is the clutter of life that distorts and clouds the perception of the 'newborn stoic'.

It was brilliant that I went blind at the age of 8, before the clutter of my life got a look in.

Epictetus made a very good point when he said that lameness was an impediment of the leg not of the will. To my mind, I often feel that people are more disabled by their thoughts, state of mind, perception, than they are by anything physical. The most physically disabled person can often be the most capable and the most physically able the most incapable. It all comes down to 'strength of will'.

— Verity Smith, a blind international dressage rider, singer, songwriter and author.

She has represented Great Britain in the Paralympics, and is now training with the aim of qualifying for the 2020 Tokyo games to fulfill her dream of competing on the Able Bodied Team.

Human Nature

"What bothers me about the emotionless cow thing is that it regards Stoicism as being primarily about emotional regulation. Getting clear about the emotions was certainly part of the picture for ancient Stoics, but it's not the key to their system, not at all.

For them, the main thing was to get clear about human nature: what it is to be a rational creature, what is our place in the universe and how we connect to one another.

It was their view that both we and our world are products of intelligent design. From that, it follows that if there's a capability that belongs to human nature, there should be a right use for that capability. And the capacity to feel deeply, to be elated or eager or even horrified, is indeed part of our nature. The trick is to get our values right so that the things we react strongly to are the ones that truly matter for a human being.

Once a person learns to care intensely about honesty, courage, and compassion, and only provisionally about their income or their reputation or even how long they live, then the emotions, too, fall into line. But getting there is hard – it could be a lifelong project."

— Margaret Graver, one of the best known and respected scholars on Stoicism and ancient philosophy.

She is the author of the popular academic text Stoicism and Emotion, in which she disproves the myth of Stoicism as a philosophy advocating being emotionless. Currently, she is the Aaron Lawrence Professor in Classics at Dartmouth, where she offers a variety of courses on Greek and Roman Philosophy, Plato, Aristotle, and Latin literature.

Stoic Realism

"Seneca can sound at times like he is quoting a passage from Scripture, particularly when he exhorts people to remember their death. I love the line in one of Seneca's letters, "Old and young alike should have death before their eyes; we are not summoned in order of birth registration."

I am not surprised that Stoicism is experiencing a modern-day revival. The Stoic emphasis on living in accord with reason and virtue is very much lacking today. And I think everyone could benefit from embracing more Stoic realism rather than reasoning solely according to our passion.

Personally, I find the Stoic emphasis on self-discipline and realism to be inspiring and helpful in my spiritual life."

Made in the USA
Middletown, DE
25 September 2023

39225439R00071